i witness

partial observations

Kapil Sibal

IndiaInk
ROLI BOOKS

for

my mother
who gifted me
my life

my father
who taught me
what it meant

my grandson
who makes me
relive the gift

Contents

Acknowledgements

The initial printed draft represented a product not yet launched. It had to be polished and window dressed. I needed to share this private journey as I moved towards publication. The joy of writing is essentially personal. But the task of publication involves many players. There are those who brainstorm about certain words and sentences; others deal with the format and yet others in the execution and design of the book. The quality of their involvement is perhaps as intense as the act of writing. I have been singularly lucky with friends who made this happen, as I had little time to devote towards finalizing this book. Realizing my predicament, my friends took it upon themselves to tie up the loose ends.

Without Khushwant's encouragement this would have been a draft in my drawer. He was most gracious in his offer to have it published. The couple of evenings spent with him were memorable. I will always cherish those moments. He is the one who suggested Roli Books as we discussed other possibilities. I am indebted to Reeta Devi for persuading me to show my work to Khushwant Singh. She has been supportive of this venture from its inception.

Apart from the family, Mala Singh and her husband Jugnu were my first victims. Mala's persona is larger than life. She has the ability to either dampen your spirits or make you fly high, depending on her mood. That evening, at their house, she was overwhelmingly responsive. Without her unstinted support, this book would not have been possible.

I thank Pavan Verma for his comments on the manuscript and his open offer to help.

I am deeply touched by Namita Gokhale's incisive comments and gentle persuasions in re-orienting some of my thoughts. Her editorial inputs have enhanced the quality of the presentation. I also thank her research assistant, Shubhda Khanna, for the help she extended.

Shumita Didi-Sandhu got involved in the project when she heard a few of my poems. While discussing some themes, I realized that she was the ideal person to understand my thought processes as they evolved. As we went through each poem, she offered detailed comments – both substantive and editorial. These reflected the essence of what I wished to convey. But for her patience, nudging me to work and re-work, this final version would not have been possible. Shumita did not relent till the outcome was to her satisfaction. Her contribution is truly invaluable.

Rajesh R., my secretary had the most difficult task to perform. He had to spend long hours transcribing the anthology and occasionally, with some hesitation, corrected me. I have, in the last two months, realized that one should have the capacity to learn from everyone. This has, in some way, humbled me. My deep gratitude to him for smiling even though he was at the receiving end – grappling with my moods, impatient to give those endless final touches. I will always remember his patience and dedication.

I also wish to thank Nirmal Singh and Azam Mian, who overheard some of what I had written, and quietly smiled without comment.

The absent presence of my late wife, Nina Sibal, permeates many of the poems. My sons, Amit and Akhil, though not entirely convinced, still encouraged me to publish. My daughters-in-law, Pavani and Shivani were effusively forthcoming.

I thank Geetanjali, Anuradha and Priya for cheering me on.

Promila, my wife, is the one who suffered the most. She sportingly put up with lack of communication during long periods of my use of the cell phone. Sometimes I was in 'silent' mode. At other times, my pre-occupied vacant expression evoked an indulgent response. I am grateful for her deep affection and enormous capacity to be patient. She willingly resigned herself to hearing some of the poems, ad nauseum. Her dry wit and culinary skills always provided me with the necessary sustenance to carry on.

I wish to express my gratitude to my publisher, Roli Books, Pramod Kapoor and Priya Kapoor for reposing confidence in me.

Introduction

This has turned out to be an unintended venture. Over the years, I wrote occasionally, but almost always in rhyme. As president of the Supreme Court Bar, whenever a judge retired I often gifted him a poem, duly framed, about his tenure – mostly appreciative of his performance. I believe that this biased memorabilia is still cherished by some. At the Bar, the golden rule, in order to seek discretionary relief, is to be exceptionally laudatory about the judges. I did not, after their retirement want to deviate from this well-accepted norm.

I would sometimes pen my thoughts on loose sheets of paper, which invariably got lost. Some, that I was able to retrieve were saved by others. Most of my prized possessions were misplaced while shifting residences. Composing a poem requires time and private space, but as years went by, both became a scarce commodity. However, significant events evoked in me the desire to put my thoughts down. Pen and paper proved to be a tedious medium, given the fact that my mind moved faster than my fingers and so the scribble at the end was sometimes illegible. I needed an easier medium through which I could express myself.

The cell phone was like a dream come true. I could write while travelling and in relative privacy, without the embarrassment of others looking over my shoulder. It also allowed me to see a legible version without having to fret and fume at my often – indecipherable ruminations.

One day while on a two-and-a-half-hour long flight, I put my cell phone on offline mode and started entering random thoughts. I had been wanting to write for a long time, especially after being exposed to a wide variety of issues, which are not only matters of public concern but have agitated my mind over the years. I started writing about different subjects ranging from nano technology to the stillness of nature after a rain shower.

This innovative medium allowed me to embark upon a new journey. It took on a life of its own. Images and experiences embedded in the recesses of my mind came alive. Apart from the world of politics around me, and the enormous possibilities of emerging technologies, my exciting years in the legal profession and my love for cricket along with some intimate moments of my life were easily expressed in digital form.

The essence of a thought can be expressed succinctly in blank verse, but for me, the rhythm of rhyme is more attractive. It also enables me to put things in better perspective and has a lyrical quality, which is a source of great joy. Many of my thoughts could have been essays or middles. But, instinctively, poetry allowed me to express myself in a more focused manner, without having to write long-winded prose.

I hesitated to share a few of these 'partial observations' with family and close friends, concerned that their honest opinion may just turn out to be a dampener. Those close to me have always been constructively critical and brutally honest. That they largely enjoyed what I wrote emboldened me to share some of my poems with Khushwant Singh. He published a few excerpts in his celebrated column, 'With Malice Towards One And All'. That for me was the turning point.

Most of my reflections are personal concerns about contemporary society. There is no intended malice here. The only poem that relates to an individual is the one on Atalji. It is part of the record of the proceedings of the Rajya Sabha, as I quoted it in one of the debates. The 'Man behind the Mask' will always remain an enigma. I can't help feeling that of them all, he is the tallest. His ambivalence about some of the strident positions his Party took, came through. Even when he was quiet, his body language spoke. History is yet to pass judgement on his leadership.

Sometimes musings assume life-like proportions. The written thought gains a momentum of its own and the emerging form has often taken me by surprise. I have thoroughly relished this roller-coaster ride especially since political commitments and my official responsibilities left very little time for such an exciting adventure.

I share this with you tentatively and hope that you enjoy reading it.

Nostalgia

I miss the smell of burning waste,
the wake-up call of temple bells,
and vendors whom I chatter with,
bargaining as they sell.

Dusty winds, scorching sun,
the odour of a busy street,
guzzling cool juices,
restless to beat the heat.

Chassis tilted to one side,
vintage buses chug along. 1
Sweaty and a smoky ride
is how it carries on.

Whistling sound of empty taps,
trickling water buckets fill.
Daily travails of summer time
through a repetitive drill.

Monsoon showers wash away
dried up dust from rusty trees;
thirsty nature, lush and green,
sways gently with the breeze.

Thatched roofs dripping in the night,
pools of water, choked up drains;

flooded streets and stranded cars;
cyclists, wading through rain.

The poor solemnly stare in space,
the seasons take their toll each year;
those impoverished, yet again
forever live in fear.

Diwali, with its fireworks,
lights up the winter skies;
time for universal brotherhood,
renewing family ties.

Cool breeze and soft winter chill
huddle in close embrace;
silhouette of contorted forms
around a crackling fireplace.

As the haze of winter lifts
and nature turns around,
I think of all the sights I miss
when I am outward bound.

Scars of Hope

Layers of cladding, if peeled,
expose barriers, I do confess,
concealing secrets within,
hoping that others might guess.

Each passing day, we artfully hide
the hurt that simmers within,
unable to face, choosing to ignore,
despair over what might have been.

Scars, like history, carry a tale
of events that impact our life.
Stories untold, we wish to unfold,
discard with a surgeon's knife.

Morning sun eclipses the night
helps us clean up the mess;
each day a celebration of life
starts with a gentle caress.

Dichotomy

I am not free,
nor do I
want to be.
Freedom, for me,
is a conceptual
fallacy.

I am what I am,
not because
I was free.
I am moulded,
enslaved,
circumstantially.

A relative term,
freedom, depends
upon capacity.
Economic power
and human
sagacity.

Do not want
freedom, as
defined for me.
Real freedom
comes with
mortality.

In the Lap of Heaven

I was born
into this world,
my mother's lap was luxury.
Without a care
I suckled away,
fussed about indulgently.

Short rapid movements;
stretched my legs,
woke up reluctantly.
Blissful days
and nights went by,
gazing wondrously.

The deft touch
of gentle skin
caressed me lovingly.
Wrapped my hands
and tightly held
all offers made to me.

When I gurgled,
familiar faces
looked on dotingly.
Kissed all over,
my hands and feet,
whispered, cooing at me.

Then I learnt
of sounds I knew,
I mouthed often with glee.
Ma and pa,
I was convinced,
were only meant for me.

Passed all tests
without exams,
none said 'no' to me.
Then one day
I realized,
this was just fantasy.

I had to learn
of right and wrong,
I was no longer free.
And what I
for granted took,
it was not meant to be.

For those of us
who have it good,
our icons of prosperity.
No comfort matches
this cushion of love,
in the lap of luxury.

The Lioness

The raging lioness often kills
to feed its hungry pride,
teaching cubbies how to hunt
as they frolic by her side.
As adults when on their own,
her lessons are a guide:
let all beasts live in harmony,
kill only to survive.

Laxmi entered her second home –
an accommodating, demure bride.
Macho men, Herculean feats
sought to be glorified.
Protectors of the weaker sex
– been worshipped, deified,
such patriarchal images
unfairly justified.

Laxmi, leitmotif of our lives,
for centuries tongue-tied,
sold with cattle, other wares
devalued, ossified.
Shakti, Saraswati, Parvati,
all virtues personified,
like a colossus she will rise
to see the turn of tide.

Wishing to live in harmony,
she is our precious pride.
Lioness of our civilized world,
without her we won't survive.

Human Predators

In the midst of this eternal expanse,
planet Earth, a speck in space,
homo sapiens' only home
in our galaxy's vast embrace.

This habitat we call our home
evolved to near perfection;
human acts endanger it –
a globally shared perception.

Majestic mountains, draped in white;
let dancing waters flow –
deep crevices, wounded terrain,
stark nature's fulsome glow.

Burning cauldron deep within
like frothing lava flows;
outpourings of a tortured world,
its mysteries no one knows.

Our ignorant defaulting ways
have brought us to the brink.
Endangered species numbers grow
while others are extinct.

Carbon emissions are the cause
for temperatures to surge.
When swelling ocean waters rise
vast tracts of land submerge.

Small island states and coastal lands,
where millions choose to live,
witness nature's relentless wrath,
reluctant to forgive.

Polluted rivers, dried up streams,
cause for acute distress;
depleted aquifers will trigger
a global water stress.

Droughts and floods impact those
who struggle to survive,
the devastation caused thereby
saps their will to live.

In warmer climes, spread of disease
both virulent, unknown –
bruised nature will avenge itself
for reasons that are known.

Denuding forests, felling trees,
destroying top soils errantly.
Nature's lungs will fail to breathe,
impacting human destiny.

The eco-system's splendid wonders
governed by nature's flawless lays,
let them not be torn asunder
by brazen man's exploiting ways.

Wrath

Swirling winds
around the eye of a storm,
gather momentum
as they move on –
with uncharted
velocity, much like
man's ferocity;
leaving destruction
in its wake,
celebrating violence
for its sake.

I never have understood
why so many of us
have to die.

Tsunami

Ocean waves
seen receding
deceptively

Innocent children
running forth
expectantly

Swelling waters
devour them
effortlessly

Spreading panic
and havoc
ruthlessly

Washing away
unrealized dreams
unjustly

Broken homes
unfinished lives
unexpectedly

Without hope
gather courage
audaciously

Rebuild lives
once again
fearfully

Human spirit
on display
breathtakingly

Lost ones
roam around
aimlessly

Others drift
into despair
understandably

Dealing with
open wounds
sensitively

Human tragedy
evokes response
globally

Financial aid
is forthcoming
copiously

NGOs
rebuild lives
tirelessly

Warning systems
to be built
immediately

Nature targets
the unprotected
remorselessly

Senseless injustice
a monumental
tragedy

Human spirit
shall resurrect
triumphantly

Death

Eternal silence, immobile
with memories left behind,
unexplained, enforced serenity,
attribution to acts divine.

Flashes of a life gone by,
etched in tissues of the mind;
innocent targets victimized,
the wrath of nature blind.

Festering wounds,
destined to heal,
will take a little time.
Death, the greatest leveller,
is difficult to define.

Mirage

How can we
all equal be?
That is the human
tragedy.

In unequal
circumstances
born, unequal
we shall be.

Unequal stations
in our lives,
reason for
inequality.

Equality of
faculties, not
a genetic
reality.

Equality of
opportunities,
gives unequals
parity.

A constitutional
guarantee?
No panacea
for inequality.

Scraping the Sky

Stark cold structures
rupture aesthetics
high on technology
plush and luxurious
payments usurious
designer ecology

Inanimate lifeless
geometric and heartless
breaching the blue sky
architecturally spineless
supinely listless
eternally dry

Such structures ignoble
culture now global
whither art and tradition
we need to preserve
our cultural curves
with modern rendition

Unknown Continent

The icy veins
of that frozen world
are witness to
antiquity.

Antarctica –
it beckons us.
We must just
let it be.

Ocean white
in recesses harsh
hide creation's
mysteries.

Disembowelling
efforts will
impact
rapaciously.

Follow the Ice

Phoenix landed on planet Mars
four score million miles –
a journey to another world
to trace out cosmic life.

Endured extreme temperatures
through Martian atmosphere,
perilously plunged to surface red,
singular feat we proudly cheer.

Travelling at enormous speed,
touch down at five mph;
NASA watched with bated breath
the 'seven minute terror stretch'.

Metallic feats in outer space
performed with use of parachute,
shedding heat-sheet and backshell,
firing twelve thrusters, to boot.

Transformation from spacecraft
to a robotic research station;
solar panels, spread out wide,
provide power at destination.

The valley of northern latitudes
hosts water rich permafrost;

glimpse of unexplored frontiers
no matter how high the cost.

Piercing through synthetic eyes
our galaxy we scan,
conquering virgin frontiers,
increase our knowledge span.

Searching for the reason why,
where and how it all began,
look for microbial signatures;
the eternal quest of man.

Road to Extinction

Jellyfish are brainless beings
but nature's ancient pride,
translucently move tentacles
to stun and paralyze.

With these elusive creatures
who multiply and breed,
Mediterranean coasts stand
deluged and besieged.

Turtles and sharks vanishing,
with tuna shoals on wane,
resurgence of these jellyfish,
causes concern and pain.

Depleted aqua vertebrates
have sadly fallen prey
to man's insensitive and
avid consuming ways.

This mindless dredging of
mighty oceans and seas,
with hungry nets the size
of massive football fields.

Time for us to pause and think,
our eco-system is out of sync.

In a Clinch

In retrospect, it was a slip
for having bought a single clip.
Had I known you won't say 'no'
I would have brought you clips galore.

What to buy? I thought a lot
of many things you haven't got
and yet in memory of this trip
I came back with a single clip.

It'll hold your locks and keep in place
ruffled thoughts, like hair in face;
and when with vision clear you look,
you'll see a man, like an open book.

In a flash, you will then find
that memories are left far behind;
at timely moments clips, when used,
clear the mind so oft confused.

Lean back, relax, let mind afloat,
forget for a moment what I wrote;
my image in your mind let slip
and stick there like a single clip.

Lovers and the Chowkidar

Every time you met me,
your arrival woefully late,
I stood, somewhat embarrassed,
outside your college gate.

Those who saw me waiting
smiled knowingly at me,
a sight that they had witnessed
ever so frequently.

You noticed not my protests
and with an open smile
expressed regret, that yet again
I'd waited for a while.

We waited for the sun to set
to hold each other tight;
nocturnal prowl, the chowkidar,
sentinel of the night.

Spotted with his flashy torch
both in dishevelled state,
ensuring that potential sinners
must never fall from grace.

These oft repeated encounters
between the chowkidar and us

left us desperate and frustrated;
we wondered why the fuss.

But, familiar with his tactics,
his surreptitious moves,
our sixth sense always warned us,
plus the squeaking of his shoes.

Like soldiers on the border
forever changing track;
committed to our mission,
prepared for a surprise attack.

Fatigued, he lay down his arms;
the chowkidar realized why
two innocent youthful lovers
escape the vigilant eye.

Utopia

Neither time
nor age
touches you,
for my mind
keeps you
evergreen.

Like a freshly
painted canvas
of memories,
a celebration
of love that
might have been.

You Left Me Midway

I still reach out to touch
the texture of your skin
unmindful of the years gone by,
the emptiness within.

Many things you left unsaid,
our dialogue incomplete;
I need another chance, my love,
wonder when next we'll meet.

Meandering and unguarded thoughts,
early morning cups of tea,
sharing both our fears and dreams
and all our fantasies.

Footprints you have left behind,
snapshots of a broken life;
sustaining us in different ways,
cherished memories survive.

Midway through our journey's end
in close embrace, you said goodbye;
though reconciled to cruel fate,
still ask the question 'why'?

My Boys

Our backyard bloomed
with just two flowers
you brought up tenderly.
Quenching their thirst
you mothered them
with nutrient energy.

Sheltered them
from scorching sun
and gusty winds of change.
Then set them free,
sturdy and young,
but life was not the same.

With moorings lost,
buffeted and scarred,
anchorless at sea,
with grit and courage,
embattled on,
securing their destiny.

They briskly walked
the path you tread
to fight adversity,
cherish to date
your abounding love
and now some more of me.

As We Approach the Night

At dusk
the evening sun
with diminishing intensity
inevitably recedes
from sight.

The glow
of abiding love,
comforting our fears
as we approach
the night.

We merge,
like melting snow,
into anonymity,
embarking on our last
solo flight.

Promise to
hold my hand,
for in this battle
I lack the strength
to fight.

Final Embrace

Our journey together
passed through
rough weather
but the moments
of sunshine
were well worth
the effort.

Your virgin desire,
search for belonging.
I lit up the fire:
restlessly looked,
innocently longing
for the answers
within you.

Lying beside me
I sensed
you were ready.
In the final embrace
your hands
were steady.

Nirvana

You left me stranded,
hopelessly inadequate,
pitifully ill-equipped,
internally consumed,
intensely bitter,
subsumed by despair.

Nerve you displayed
with quiet eloquence,
resolve of purpose,
unusual dignity,
Buddhist equanimity,
none could dare.

Unwittingly taught me
virtues of valour,
forgiveness and healing,
the final surrender,
drifting,
knowing not where.

The Art of Leaving

Very few people know
the art of letting go.

Marooned in desires,
short-sighted selfish ways,
this lifetime seems eternal,
lasts only a few days.

Mirage of presumed permanence
stokes our avarice for more;
never think of giving up till
death knocks at our door.

Obsessed with acquisitions,
without exception, know
we made a naked entry
and naked we must go.

Sunday

Every Sunday comes along
with morning cups of tea;
vacantly I stretch my legs
and jog my memory.

Reliving the days gone by:
children, jumping recklessly,
plant wet kisses all over me;
I miss them desperately.

Long for their beatific smiles,
spontaneous cackling glee,
funny tales they loved to hear,
one riding on each knee.

Trips to the zoo, another world;
they looked at, curiously,
trapezing monkeys; tigers yawn
and look on nonchalantly.

Delicious burgers, dripping fries,
smacking lips hungrily,
sweaty, fatigued and half asleep,
we dozed off peacefully.

Now deadweight on my bed,
scanning papers lazily;
vacantly I stretch my legs,
remember nostalgically.

Twenty20

Splashes of colour,
a rush of blood:
the twenty20 game.
Power packed drama,
triumph and trauma:
cricket is not the same!

Rapturous crowds
in frenzied cheers,
encouraged by public acclaim.
The new gladiators,
commercial predators:
this was a gentleman's game.

Brash owner's pride,
brand ambassador's catwalk,
purists view it with disdain.
Money spinner bonanza
gala extravaganza:
test cricket perhaps too tame.

Fast paced action –
quick change of fortunes –
cheerleaders to entertain!
High scoring matches
acrobatic catches,
jarring for the urbane.

Cricket lovers' nightmare,
slapstick tamasha,
connoisseurs often complain.
Instant stroke-play
without any foreplay:
this is not cricket, they claim!

Universal Mom

My darling mom
had always dreamt
her son to be, some day
a medical doctor,
or an engineer,
one who would lead the way.

I had no heart
to tell her that, mother
you should let me be.
My mind goes numb
when confronted with
my bête noire, trigonometry.

Give me a simple
sum to solve
and I am all at sea.
Calculus, algebra
cause embarrassment
and acute mental agony.

All those with
engineering skills
have love for geometry.
My world should
have no angles,
no signs of symmetry.

Constantly harassed
medical practitioners,
I would rather a patient be.
Have no desire to
spend long years
learning bio-chemistry.

Agonizing, preparing
for brutal exams,
where ulcers are for free.
Wish not to spend
my balance years
dealing with human misery.

Help me be my engineer,
let me 'doctor' my
un-chartered destiny.
I know, dear mom,
you love me lots,
but do not plan for me.

Am aware that you want
me to lead the way
but I know what is good for me.
You led your life,
gave me this world,
don't steer my life for me.

My Very Own Journey

A villain of your
shattered dreams
I do not want to be.
The dreams I have,
if I fall short, are
my responsibility.

Close to your heart
you keep alive your
expectations of me.
I wake up nights,
break into sweat,
fear the failure I could be.

I have my shadow
by my side, your
shadow I cannot be.
I am your footprint
left behind, yet my path
will be chosen by me.

As I learn to walk, be my guide;
at the right moment
please set me free.
I hope to decide
as the canvas is wide,
creating a future for me.

At the end of the journey
I will remember you pa
for always thinking of me,
I chartered my life
through moments of strife,
this is how it had to be.

Unending Shuffle

We take the system for a ride.
Exploiting it, we live our lives.
In all our ventures must ensure
that two plus two makes five.

Brokers tips for bullish stocks;
tax haven and Mauritius route!
Windfall profits in real estate;
insider trading, corporate loot.

In our complex financial world,
the rich have thirst for more.
Hedonistic spiralling prosperity:
with enough cushion to store.

When the going is truly tough
and time has come to share,
they are the first to criticize,
ask governments to beware.

Investor friendly policies
and interest rates be low.
Foreign direct investments:
constant stream of capital flow.

A corporate global regime,
low wages are the key.

Monopolists make quick profits,
not meant for you and me.

Continuing at their mercy,
hoping for better days.
The tragedy of Sisyphus
not just a passing phase.

Sisyphus: In Greek mythology, Sisyphus was the son of King Aeolus of Thessaly and Enarete, and the founder and first king of Ephyra (Corinth). He was being punished in Tartarus by being cursed to roll a huge boulder up a hill, only to watch it roll down again, and to repeat this throughout eternity. Today, Sisyphean can be used as an adjective meaning that an activity is unending and/or repetitive. It could also be used to refer to tasks that are pointless and unrewarding.

Inflation

Inflation is
much in the news,
fodder for many
differing views.

Inflationary products,
when in use,
have attributes
somewhat obtuse.

Inflationary trends
might lead to harm,
inflated values
signal alarm.

Let us examine
and ascertain
if all inflation
is cause for blame.

Inflated balloons
surreptitiously fly,
like unmanned spies
up in the sky.

Inflated egos,
insufferable folk

become a butt of
many a joke.

Inflated tyres
of obesity,
sure recipe
for calamity.

Inflated prices:
rank profiteer.
Inflated books
of a racketeer.

Inflated bunny,
sexual delight,
poor substitute for
a lonely night.

Inflated stomach,
belching concern,
requires visiting
an intern.

Inflated premiums
help sustain
frequently inflated
insurance claims.

Inflated stocks
are traded high,
sharp brokers know
the reasons why.

Prices of goods in
short supply
begin to rise
when demand is high.

Market dynamics
cause outcry,
we must explain
the reasons why.

Food-grain production
slowly plateaued;
global population
in upward mode.

Australia suffered
unexpected drought:
global prices
knocked about.

Galloping consumption
of steel is proof

why input prices
have hit the roof.

Edible oils:
growing demand;
we don't possess
a magic wand.

Remain committed
and ensure
rising costs don't
hurt the poor.

Inflation is
bound to abate
with corrective steps
sooner than late.

Futile to rock this sailing boat
the rising tide will keep afloat.

Shameless

Rapacious culture
of our times,
we embrace with alacrity
'dog eat dog' as
we move ahead;
ask 'what's in it for me'?

Hoping to get a
substantial raise in
our six figure salary,
with cash thrown in
and perks to boot,
is the hike we want to see.

Reluctant employees
who milch the state
look for more freebies,
lucrative postings with
discretionary powers,
a host of possibilities.

Floating agents, who
help close deals,
manipulate artfully;
claim, when done,
their pound of flesh;
no service is ever for free.

Those committed to
our ambitious endeavours
ask us repeatedly:
'sir, what have we got,
after so many years of
backing you constantly'.

For all that we do,
there is a price to be paid,
trading on integrity.
Those without means
ask for nothing, except
a window of opportunity.

Politician's Eightfold Path

A Public Perception of a Noble Species

Embrace his ignoble Eightfold Path,
the footprint of salvation.
Obstacles run over with
ruthless determination.

Righteous View allows you to,
for every public action,
line your pocket appropriately
for total satisfaction.

For Right Intent, recognise
the passion for acquisition.
Such a sense of purpose
must inform your every decision.

Right Speech is to serve you well;
communicate the truth
about others in chaste language,
though abusive and uncouth.

Right Action shuns abstinence,
leading to deprivation,
encouraging all those brokers,
helping in wealth creation.

Intoxicants and weapons trade,
fundamentals of Right Livelihood.

Embracing such activity
leads to untold private good.

Right Effort is misguided
energy and brute force.
Rise above moral issues;
unwholesomeness endorse.

Right Mindfulness is cognition
imperfect and derailed,
where action is uncontrolled
and conscience is for sale.

Right Conscience is a mental force
where ends must serve the means;
integrity is compromised,
immorality supreme.

This ignoble Eightfold Path,
the golden rule for some –
unmindful of our destiny
and of our freedoms won.

Eightfold Path: The Buddha laid down the Noble Eightfold Path, a way to end the suffering. It is a practical guideline to ethical and mental development with the goal to free the individual from attachments and delusions; and it finally leads to understanding the truth about all things.

Refraction

The rainbow of democracy,
with subtle shades and hues;
a form of government that absorbs
conflicting differing views.

Founded on electoral politics
free expression of your choice;
hoping that, in this process,
we have a cohesive voice.

Disparate elements forge together
unsteady coalitions, a quick fix;
ideological positions take a beating,
looking for political gimmicks.

Buffeted by constituents
who seek out personal gain;
crowing that they made you win,
feel entitled to lay claims.

Power hungry merchants seek
a billion different things;
national picture comes unstuck;
realpolitik begins.

Issues, systems and the like
are given least priority;

decision making influenced for
securing a majority.

Outcry of bewilderment,
search for cohesive voice;
where colours of the rainbow
will be matters of our choice.

Political Opportunism

A somersault is
a turnabout with
acrobatic skills;
for those who
watch admiringly, it
does not cease to thrill.

The supple flowing
twists and turns, a
challenge to static ways;
a quick change of
positions, endearing
artistic displays.

For those of us who
somersault, in gauche
and awkward style;
must learn to do it
with panache, but
that will take a while.

Without practice if
you somersault, you
might fall flat on face;
without the artful
use of words, look
helpless and disgraced.

Practice along with
reason, helps
somersault with ease,
those contradictory
postures, will not
threaten to displease.

Sycophant
An Endearing Indian Phenomena

As I see him from afar,
I weave my way to greet him,
deftly manoeuvre my every step,
lest I fail to meet him.

When he walks, I follow suit
and as he changes direction
I suitably choreograph my way
almost to perfection.

Perchance a glance, a turn of head
and when he looks my way,
that is the time, with folded hands,
I greet him with 'namaste'.

Not wasting time, I tell him of
the speech that he had made,
of gestures, carefully crafted words,
and maturity displayed.

The notes were apt, a chord was struck
the frenzied crowd I thought
utterly charged, by words unsaid
that was the best onslaught.

The leader smiled, my day was made.
I half lay on the ground,

supinely moved a few steps back,
and weaved my way around.

My leader is thoughtful and kind,
makes me feel most wanted;
endangered species that he is,
I can't take him for granted.

Erroneous Zone

I got up to argue the case
trying to read the Judge's face.
Expressionless; conveyed to me,
was eager to dismiss my plea.

Told him, of the findings made
dehors the evidence, and
laid before him facts to show
the errors of the courts below.

He stated, while in appeal
argue not with extra zeal;
that lower courts had plainly found
against my client, thus he was bound.

The law he said was very clear
this court's not meant to interfere.

Ab Ovo Ad Finem

Justice is a teasing goal,
eluding all seeking perfection;
those charged with administering it
require a course correction.

Access to courts, a universal right,
beyond the common reach;
millions are left without recourse
as basic rights are breached.

Good lawyering is on the wane,
some kith and kin hold sway,
and moneybags oft move the court,
manoeuvring for a stay.

Indigent victims, waiting, lie
as justice goes astray;
backlogs overwhelm the judge:
clients still have to pay.

Unending saga of distress,
solutions we must find;
we need a change of status quo,
deliver justice as divined.

Under the Carpet

Our public has a right to know.
With the RTI now in force,
public servants must disclose
acquired assets and their source.

Transparency in public life:
recognized democratic norm.
Strict enforcement will ensure
much anticipated reform.

Judges are public servants, too.
Declared by courts, thus far
they have no special privileges,
all public servants at par.

Disclosure of Judges' assets
to Chief Justice of India,
knowing not how he intends
scrutinizing precious data.

Would like him to hand over
to an agency of repute,
investigate such disclosures,
if suspect or in dispute.

If this system has not worked,
we need to think afresh;

calls for institutional change
and not to window dress.

Festering wound of corruption
needs a new approach, because
you know it is not right to be
a Judge in your own cause.

RTI: Right to Information Act 2005

Chaste and Haste

My Lord, I wish to make a point:
the law is seldom an ass.
When sometimes it is,
where ignorance is bliss,
all I can say is alas!

The judges of yore,
well versed in the law,
seldom dismissed in haste.
But did on occasion,
despite persuasion,
their logic, impeccably chaste.

Our accomplished Lords
now on the bench,
most eager to dismiss the brief,
seize procedural lapse,
which leads to collapse,
and the client is put to grief.

Delivery of justice,
a godly endeavour,
requires both time and space.
The parties must feel
they were dealt a fair deal –
helps justice falling from grace.

Uncommon Bedfellows

Sometimes I wonder
what journalists and lawyers
have in common.
The answer seems clear:
both professional disciplines
represent parasitic phenomena.

One investigates to satiate
the thirst of readers, hungry
for a newsworthy report.
The other spins out a story
for delivery of justice in court.

Both dissect through minutiae
to weave a credible version.
More often than seldom,
salacious details
evoke frenetic discussion.

Feeding on enervated targets
with intent to defend
(often the indefensible),
these pretenders of the faith
are frequently undependable.

Vestiges of Sanity

Reasonableness of
thought and
purity of action
are hallmarks
of sobriety.

Both are drawn
unashamedly upon
by those who
seek to justify
acts of impropriety.

The application
of reason
to support a set
of dubious conclusions
leads to notoriety.

Purity of action
adulterated motives
subvert, the
raison d'etre of
civilized society.

Courts of law
which epitomize

purity of thought
reasonableness of action
alone provide

An illusion of hope.

Gist

Belief
sans reason
is faith.

Blind faith
most religions
propagate.

Religious leaders
with preaching
captivate.

Young minds
obsessive passion
invigorate.

Conforming values
for all others
to emulate.

Breeding ground
for prejudice
and hate.

Hard won freedoms
will eventually
suffocate.

The battle is
at our doorstep
don't hesitate.

Fight for reason
before it is
too late.

For reason alone
will bring on board
misguided fate.

Whither Press

Free press,
challenged today
by corporate world.

Making news
like other products
commercially sold.

Advertising revenue
drives content
for gratification.

Commercial interests
shamelessly receive
undue articulation.

Electronic media,
through images,
that sensationalize.

In the process,
their credibility
seriously jeopardize.

Bollywood geeks,
cricket icons,
make headline news.

What stars foretell
con-men tricks
meant to enthuse.

TRPs of channels,
soap operas,
get hits for you.

News that matters
serious content,
of limited value.

Online information,
instant coffee,
no time to brew.

Real meaty stories
bypassed
without much ado.

Opinions crafted
with analysis
rarely see.

A responsible press,
an oddity
and far from free.

To Trust or Not to Trust
2008

22nd of July
a day to remember
for both betrayal
and trust.
We won the Motion
in the midst
of commotion
the victory
clearly robust.

The betrayal came
with the chanting
of shame,
alleging that
voters were bought;
the proceedings
were tainted
for all those
acquainted, said,
the result be
set at naught.

The day was historic
the government
euphoric, the battle
decidedly tough.

Some members thought
as the Motion
was lost, was time
to play it rough.

A crime was
committed, some
electors submitted
that they were
offered a bribe.
With the media,
in tow, this seemed
a real blow, for
all Indians who
still have some pride.

This was a sting
those targeted claimed
that the story
was a tissue of lies.
Those aggrieved
should have tried
to reach the police;
not doing so
a matter of surprise.

With two hours
to go, clearly

in the know
that the vote, was
going to be lost.
They made this
tamasha, in the
well of the House
not realizing what
it might cost.

Had they gone
to the Speaker
and informed him
about it, who would
have taken one
step at a time.
Take over the
money, have
statements recorded
and kept matters
within his confine.

That might not
have suited, for
all those who wanted
to embarrass the
government that day.
Politics lost

its veneer, as
it would appear
wads of notes
on vulgar display.

We were all
in a stupor
felt cheated and
let down, by
those we hold
in esteem.

Can't compromise
the nation by
belittling its systems
not upholding its
glory, pristine.

The government had won
democracy the loser
and politics in
utter disarray.
This temple of justice
invaded by avarice
yet the nation will
still have its way.

123

May 2008

The Indo-US nuclear deal,
now a bone of contention,
with the BJP's turn about
and the Left's apprehension.

Imperialistic designs cited
as reason for suspicion;
one hoped Left ideology had
evolved through transition.

Dismantling of the Berlin wall,
fall of the iron curtain,
no Gorbachev of Indian mould
after Basu, the future uncertain.

Nuclear plants we possess
running at half capacity;
nuclear fuel in short supply,
we hope for some sagacity.

Diverse energy options will
our national interest serve,
increase the flow of power
now on a downward curve.

Scientists of renown consider
the deal an opportunity;

stripping the denial regime
no compromise on sovereignty.

Non-proliferating votaries
now seek the right to test;
Vajpayee publicly gave it up,
put petty politics to rest.

Such coalition politics, with
opposition for its own sake,
disjuncted fractured polity,
supreme interests are at stake.

Give up your protestations to
a deal that helps us with
accessing such technologies
that enrich our knowledge grid.

123: Section 123 of the United States Atomic Energy Act of 1954, titled 'Cooperation With Other Nations', establishes an agreement for cooperation as a prerequisite for nuclear deals between the US and any other nation. Such an agreement is called a 123 Agreement. Today, the US has entered into roughly twenty-five 123 agreements with various countries.

POTA

Every time that terror strikes,
politicos raise their pitch;
with elections round the corner
they hope to strike it rich.

Convinced that these terrorists,
who personify evil,
fearful of the POTA, might
think twice before they kill.

How naïve our understanding
of the global terror drive.
Live human bombs hardly care
if they are caught alive.

Those in favour of such laws
softened their stand when they
unleashed demons at Kandahar,
though POTA was in play.

POTA was on the statute book
when terror struck Akshardham,
victimized innocent believers,
disturbed the peace and calm.

Raghunath temple and Kaluchak,
yatris on way to Amarnath:

POTA was no impediment
to the dastardly bloodbath.

Votaries of the POTA want
convictions that will stand,
confessions extracted by police
from accused upon remand.

Such laws were grossly misused
when POTA was in force.
Minors were prosecuted
with little legal recourse.

Provisions of bail, unduly harsh,
prosecutors grossly misused;
the law required their consent
without which, the Judge refused.

No liberal democracy endorses
such provisions to prosecute.
POTA the only exception,
a statement not in dispute.

Move beyond this posturing,
give politics a break.
Consider the consequences;
individual freedom is at stake.

POTA or Prevention of Terrorism Act 2002 is for prevention of and for dealing with terrorist activities.

Man behind the Mask

Dear Atalji,
I must confess
it is time to clear up
all this mess.

Let us complete
unfinished tasks
and see the man
behind the mask.

December 6th,
this nation saw
gross violation
of the law.

In retrospect,
you say this meant
expression of
national sentiment.

This was a crime
against the state
stoked by anger,
venom and hate.

Qualities that
you now extol

for a short-lived
political goal.

The vote-bank
politics of BJP
is playing with
our nation's destiny.

Build that Mandir
in your heart;
let not the nation
fall apart.

Please come clean,
demonstrate that
you are still
a democrat.

Distortion

The eye
of an artist
keenly observes
etching his feelings,
no interests
he serves.

Consumers of art
amply display
support to
artistic freedom
in their own
subtle way.

Marauders
of art;
tend to disturb
the idiom of art
partisan interests
they serve.

Obscenity

Are legs,
emerging from
flappy, un-creased,
expansive knickers,
knotted with age,
spindles of antiquity,
straining energetically
for rejuvenation,
really obscene?

No more,
no less than
supple young legs,
scantily clad,
with shapely thighs,
manicured condition,
riveting attention,
seek to be
seductive.

Defining Moments

A good judge is one who:

hears everybody
but listens
only to his
conscience.

A good lawyer is one who:

rejects the
unconscionable
doubts the
improbable
respects the
probable
projects the
reasonable.

A good journalist is one who:

rejects the
reasonable
suspects the
probable
embraces the
improbable
investigates the
unconscionable.

A successful politician is one who:

makes the unconscionable
sound reasonable
and the reasonable
sound unconscionable.

Winner's Recipe

There is no recipe for
winning an election.

Some practice persuasion
others attempt deception.

Planting hostile stories
for a negative reaction.

Some accuse opponents
of callous dereliction.

And if that misfires
allege gross infraction.

Of model code of conduct
an electoral distraction.

Famous Bollywood stars
are a welcome attraction.

Manipulate gullible crowds
for theatric satisfaction.

Hunting for opportunities
for large scale defection.

Haven for practitioners of
the art of infiltration.

For non-serious supporters
a time for recreation.

Blackmailing workers
threaten with desertion.

Gun-toting thugs
instruments of coercion.

Fundamentalists at large
stoke societal dissension.

Instigating violence
cause communal tension.

Elections are no time for
sacrifice and abstention.

No time for dialogue
or time for comprehension.

Of issues of the moment
crying out for attention.

Ideologies in the dustbin
seek mafia protection.

Our fractured democracy
an act in self-delusion.

Most electoral victories
an ephemeral illusion.

Age of the Ape

A look at you and
some would think
you might provide the
Missing Link.

Eyes sullen, pug nose,
long hair on nape,
maybe there was a
Lemurian Ape.

Which over the years
became extinct;
your presence now
provides a hint.

Of this great leap
from Ape to Man,
let's understand now
what we can.

The 'ba ba's' gurgling
through your throat
homo-sapien sounds
connote.

Gorillas, when they
are on heat,

their ‘ba ba’s’ are not
as discreet.

Hairy tufts
sprouting from ears,
thanks to your
gorilla peers.

When trimmed,
they make you look
a live star from a
jungle book.

Pigmented skin, flat
concave face,
long arms, short legs,
gorilla’s grace.

And when in sporting
jest you play,
we must call it
‘gorilla day’.

You do us proud
‘oh hairy one’,
I wonder how it
had all begun.

The world today is
out of shape,
let us rejoice
Age of the Ape.

Smooth Sailing

Our bureaucrats
have finely tweaked
Newton's famous
Law of Motion.

Positive actions
must be opposed,
with a robust
negative reaction.

Policy prescriptions,
when in place, the
minister states them
with clarity.

They slow down
movement of the files,
taking recourse in
Law of Gravity:

Those requiring
urgent action
kept at the bottom
of the pile.

Prepare a detailed
string of objections

which actions
cannot reconcile.

Convoluted
archaic rules
not understanding
simple facts;

Persuade the minister
to invoke
omnibus
powers to relax;

Then opine
that such authority,
if he dares
to ever use,

Has the potential of
making him
a suspect;
if not, an accused.

Most of our
national projects
will acquire enough
maturity with time.

Moving forward
at a snail's pace,
given the
bureaucratic mind.

At the time
of implementation,
all essential
parameters change:

Bureaucrats then
advise the minister
to start
all over again.

The Great Divide

The brave new world
appears flat to some
using highways in meta-space:
no brick nor mortar,
only search engines,
portals and interface.

Where information flows
in the near-real world
all in seamless display;
constantly connected
through a slew of ideas
riding a virtual highway.

Putting knowledge to use,
with unmatched skills,
the monopoly of only a few –
that makes the terrain
uneven, not plain,
causing a schism
between me and you.

Uneven World

Globalization: a catchy word,
its meaning still unclear;
for some it brings prosperity
while others live in fear.

Lower tariffs, expanding trade
neo-liberals will rejoice –
free flow of consumer goods,
the luxury of choice.

Designer brands are on display
at plush malls and in boutiques,
glitzy and up-market stores,
for money market freaks.

Symbols of a flattened world
where the global rich unite,
interact in seamless ways:
a pretty ugly sight.

Those of us four billion strong,
living shades of poverty,
ours is an uneven world
of squalor, want and misery.

Where children of a lesser God
work for daily sustenance,

scavengers in a global world
where virtue is in abstinence.

Schooling is a distant goal
and dropouts are a norm.
Doctors' fees are hard to pay;
dazed mothers look forlorn.

Many ride the global wave
the Buffetts and the Gates;
all others, watching wistfully,
surrender to their fates.

Meeting in London

I dread to meet,
at Oxford street,
the same old faces
exchanging usual graces,
backslapping each other –

'How are you brother,
enjoying the weather?'

'All family together
away from the heat,
holiday complete,
and wife is busy
on shopping tizzy,
makes her happy!
Buying for child,
they all going wild,
picking up clothing
almost for nothing!

Best part is, sir,
this is like ghar.
London is great,
like Indian state,
every summer coming,
pleasant and cooling,
old friends meeting,

together eating
idli and dosa
– also stuffed samosa.'

An ideal vacation,
no cultural dislocation.

Paradigm Shift

Geo-spatial images in
digital mode display
enabling introspection
in a most effective way.

Remote sensing satellites
with resolutions high
map the global surface
from a geo-spatial sky.

Geo-spatial technologies
with an IT interface
video-graph in real-time
three dimensional space.

Integrating data
on geo-spatial terrain
with multifarious uses
in the public domain.

Geo-spatial products
sold for commercial gain
by multinational entities
on the NY stock exchange.

Geo-spatial software skills
architectural designs

engineering challenges
confront futuristic minds.

Geo-spatial solutions are
the new emerging art
usage of visual texture
inter-active and smart.

Unique geo-spatial footprints
accessed through the net
convergence of technologies
impacting our mindset.

Exciting knowledge era
possibilities untold
use IT BT processes
in a geo-spatial world.

BT: Biotechnology

Live Memories

Write me not
a quick SMS
professing that
you love me.

I do not want
to be erased
this quickly from
your memory.

I'd rather have
your written word,
in long hand,
your very own.

To remind you of
the feelings that
you later
might disown.

Dried up ink
still keeps afresh,
loving memories
bound to last.

You can't erase
the written word,

cannot tear off
the past.

Digital words
distinguish not
the writer of
the script.

Does not convey
the nervousness,
when emotions
are adrift.

Want the fragrance
of your words,
may be on
a tattered sheet.

To keep alive
the love professed,
whenever
we will meet.

Elysian Fields

Monsoon showers wash away
oppressive summer heat;
expectant nature springs to life,
just like the way we meet.

Tortured landscape hoping
for the rain to quench its thirst.
Every time you meet me, love,
it always seems the first.

Effigies of a love that left
scarred imprints on your mind:
cautiously we move along
a path not yet defined.

As with nature, seasons change,
new spring is in the air,
tender buds aching to bloom,
we nurture them with care.

Pitter Patter

Rain of this intensity
has a softness about it
that is almost feminine.
And your pitter patter
is as soft as raindrops.

Changing course
in a gentle current with
the clap of thunder
is nature's way of release
at the advent of summer.

A cool breeze occasionally
shoulders its way,
briskly touching your skin,
bringing cheer
to your life.

I feel like the cool breeze
touching you as you relax
and adjust your body
to let it flow,
reach the extremities
of your being.

Silence of Unspoken Words

Shall I woo you
with words
woven in
silken threads
that resonate
as you look
into my eyes?

Or will you
let me slip
into your mind
and cradle
your memories
in the comfort
of my presence?

Barriers are
like citadels
of distrust,
impregnable to
the change
of seasons
ushering hope.

Fear not the
storm surges;
the calm

in the aftermath
will stretch
the contours
of our being.

The silence of
unspoken words
overtakes us,
touching you
to savour
the new world
around.

Striking Gold

No adequate words
can help describe
the love I experienced
for years.

The language of love
has no written form,
conveyed with a smile
or with tears.

Remember the time
the mind was confused
and my yearning
would not disappear?

I could not change track;
you know how I felt,
the message was loud
and clear.

You touched me where
none did before;
I knew we had nothing
to fear.

The moments we shared
I still carry with me,

for those were times
when we dared.

The tide has not ebbed,
I still miss a beat;
the passion, my love,
is still there.

Phan Ku

Mythology has ruled our lives
and continues so to do,
foundation of abiding faith;
but most of it untrue.

600 BC, Chinese believed
Phan Ku emerged from an egg,
carved the world as we now see;
soon after, he was dead.

His skull, blue dome of the sky,
and bones, the rocks to be;
his flesh, the soil we walk upon;
blood, flowing rivers and seas.

Wind and clouds his last breath,
sweat pouring down as rain,
his hair the source of plant life
we view it with disdain.

Fleas lodged within his hair
provided a firm base
for origins of our universe
and that of the human race.

For Man to be born required
the death of his Creator,

destined by that one event,
accursed with sorrow ever after.

The myths of our disturbing times,
crumbling pillars of blind faith,
sworn enemies of reason
become instruments of hate.

Irony

Religion first
propagates
belief
then seeks to
realize it,
whereas
reason must be
the foundation of
this edifice
of faith.

Irrational belief
leads to
blind
adherence,
culminating in
a value system
which becomes
the basis of
an intolerant
society.

Yet reason has
its roots
in faith.

Faith is the
triumph of

reason and
reasonableness.

But reason
and faith
clash
when faith
jettisons reason
and reason
loses faith
in itself.

The origin of
all conflict
is either
the irrationality
of blind faith,
or reason's blind
faith in its own
infallibility.

The Terrorist

On the pyre of death,
igniting the flame of
deliverance,
I seek
salvation.

Embers of my passion
contain the essence
of hate
awaiting
germination.

Innocent victims,
participating bystanders
of this uniquely
violent
celebration.

Removed from Godliness,
yet another act of
mindless
self-inflicted
castration.

Deliverance

Violence for a terrorist
is not a means but an end.
The ultimate sacrifice for
the self to transcend.
To be one with his God:
hard put to defend
the killing of innocent
women, children and men.

T-Cells

Terrorism, a virus
incubating in
the body politic,
targeting the weak,
the vulnerable
and the innocent.

This infection
has a killer instinct,
entering the bloodstream
almost silently
and insidiously,
totally unrepentant.

Replicates itself
by inhuman intervention,
a genetically engineered
cloned product,
obsessively destructive,
violently arrogant.

Targets those
functioning organs
critically vital
to the state of harmony,
disturbing the peace,
stoking discontent.

Like the AIDS virus
mutates itself
escaping detection,
changing form,
disguises identity,
supremely self-confident.

What is required
is unity of purpose,
unbending resolve,
for the enemy
is bereft of
human sentiment.

Lease of Life

Life's a precious gift
nature provides,
absent our consent.

We have no right
to snuff it out
with capital punishment.

Should the State
ever sanctify
an act of violence?

Enforcement of
such laws, with
intent to avenge?

An eye for an eye,
a tooth for a tooth,
smacks of revenge.

Despairing victims'
families desire
a bloody end.

Deterrence a weak
rationale, difficult
to defend.

Time to have a
re-look at the
nature of punishment.

Scripted Consciousness

Misanthropic thoughts
breed hatred
for the world
and in the process
fall prey
to miseries untold.

If we choose
to look within
and script
our consciousness,
the world around
would cease to
cause the
misanthrope distress.

Within all pervasive
humankind
where open secrets lie,
the story of life itself
escapes the
misanthropic eye.

Mantra for Peace

For survival in this
violent world
the system needs
reform.

We must embrace
non-violence in
all its different
forms.

Our violence
with nature has
brought negative
returns.

Spectre of
global warming
adding to our
concerns.

Terrorism is on
the rise, founded
on cults and
hate.

To deal with it
effectively,

we need to
cogitate.

Violent means
breed violence,
leave wounds and
open scars.

A route we
have adopted
will not take us
too far.

We need an
open dialogue,
allay unfounded
fears.

Harp on universal
values all
religions hold
so dear.

Non-violence,
the only creed
will help us
to survive.

Winning of hearts
is crucial for
ending this terror
drive.

Random Thoughts

When the mist
in my mind
clears,
will, then, I
get rid of my
fears.

Religion attracts
most simple folks
who need a crutch to live;
dependent on
almighty God
with powers to
forgive.

Nature's disquiet,
expressed in
violent ways.

A subtle message
to us all, to
mend our ways.

Some wonder
how the dice
will fall.

I wonder
how He makes
the call.

Oceans are
nature's arteries,
the cauldron
within, the heart.

We are merely
beneficiaries,
without being
an integral part.

The lexicon of
nanotech, and
these are rumours
rife.

Will help provide

insights to, the
building blocks of
life.

—•—

Be youthful, foolish,
be a little mad,
don't mind the years,
just be a lad.

Catch up with time
and do not fear,
tell your children
not to interfere.

—•—

If ever I analyze
what is amiss,
most often it is
my prejudice.

Without it I cannot
fret, complain,
no one to target,
none to blame.

—•—

Our life is full of
broken dreams,
consumed by what
could have been.

We never pause
to thank dear God,
all that we have,
might not have been.

—•—

Emptiness
for me
is a way of life.

I have
a deep desire
to fill the vacuum in yours.

—•—

Gandhi taught
it is not weak
for us to turn
the other cheek.

The weak often,

through violence,
demonstrate a
show of strength.

—•—

Global warming
is a real threat;
to future generations
we owe a debt:
lest we unwittingly
jeopardize our
homo-sapient enterprise.

—•—

Atoms are
our alphabets
and molecules
our words.

Scripting them
will help us
unravel unique
worlds.

Bio-tech

Bio-tech:
scientific surgeon's knife,
genetic investigator's dream.

Opens up
a brave new world
for healthcare and well-being.

Bio-sensors
in nano forms
travel our bloodstreams.

Enter cells
of malignant tumours
heretofore not seen.

Bio-markers
to recognize
disparate qualities of genes.

Transit to
new forms of life
through revolutionary means.

Transgenics
seeks to question
nature's laws, so far supreme.

Nano

Nano tubes
in nano pores.
Nano tech
in nano stores.
Nano thoughts
of nano brains.
A plethora
of nano claims.

Nano meters,
nano miles.
Nano cars
in nano style.
In this unique
universe of ours
astronomers look
for nano stars.

Nano conflicts,
nano sites,
launching of
nano satellites,
orbiting earth both
near and far,
fear of future
nano wars.

Fresh challenges
in nano times:
investigate new
nano crimes.

Nano sensors,
nano sleuths
uncover a few
nano truths.

Nano solutions
here to stay,
living our lives
the nano way.

Nano: One-billionth (10^9)

Rising Tide

I wish that I were
in my teens,
carefree days and
tattered jeans.

And you, of twenty
years ago
an innocent lass,
all aglow.

Untouched, unspoilt
fresh, evergreen,
the discovery of
a human being.

But all's not lost
with Teesta's rage,
let's both turn over
another page.

Begin afresh,
new chapter start,
what's gone is gone
what's past is past.

Unwinding

You cannot let your hair down
with that mop on your head.
Let's start with a glass of wine
with brie and toast instead.

A glance is too inadequate;
I need to touch and feel,
to whisper in your ears about
moments I wish to steal.

Precipice

Last night, my love,
I had a dream
of having entered
your bloodstream,
extremities of which
you're not aware;
be sure, that I
have visited there.

I touched you
just beneath your skin,
seen places where
you've never been,
raced with your heart,
felt your blood flow,
never dreamt
of letting go.

Awake, I lay
in bed and thought
this journey is
with danger fraught;
we'll have to shed
our skins and leave
for places which
we can't conceive.

You know we must,
decide one day,
wake up to live
a different way.

Unshackled

Fruity, full-bodied,
deep red and more
will savour, till
I feel it flow
through nano pores,
tingling delight
blurs contours of
what's wrong or right.

My story hides
in layered seams
of a glorious life
and unfilled dreams;
all roads were paved,
the drive was straight,
each milestone a
pre-determined date.

I want a bumpy
ride today –
the time has come,
I want my way.
Constricted life
of form and grace;
I want to move
at my own pace.

Manicured lifestyles
left behind,
looking for pathways
of the mind.
Sustainable freedom
in virgin flight,
telescopic view of
wrong and right.

This life's a blip,
the journey divine,
let's start it with
a glass of wine.

Artistic Hands

Artistic hands
that touch
and mould
shape and seize
and knead
bring to life
those frozen dreams
both in and
out of bed.

Warm eyes
that stop
a world
that moves
and opens us
to share
a sensual and
pulsating life
where body
and soul are bare.

Pathfinders

Within your eyes
I want to see
the turning point
for you and me.

When I find it
I will know
that now I have
nowhere to go.

Will we get lost
in simple things
where procreating
life begins?

And treasure moments
we both find,
leaving all others
far behind?

I know we will
in years to come
start afresh,
the past undone.

Colours of My Love

Did you hear my footsteps say,
never been through this tortuous way,
where demons lurk of yesteryears,
to magnify your present fears?

Let the morning sun caress your face,
engulf you in its warm embrace;
secure within, let moments fly
and give it just another try.

The virgin present discovers true
colours of a different hue,
shades you had not seen before
will make you yearn for even more.

It's time to stop all this pretence,
to rediscover your innocence,
for knowledge is but life defiled:
the truth resides in moments wild.

When memory loses track of time
and space, like contours of the mind,
is not confined, within that state
you will forget both love and hate.

Reach within yourself and find,
discover love, leave lies behind:
mirrored in my eyes you'll see
yourself, your fate and destiny.

Shooting Star

The living cell destined to decay
begins its cycle of life;
before the last episode
seeks heavenly abode,
about which mythology is rife.

If you lead your life
in an honourable way
you might be the lucky one.
He may take you in
for committing no sin,
having lost out on all the fun.

The span of our life,
like a shooting star,
shines as it fades away.
We seek to pretend
ignoring the end –

Live cells slowly die away.

Hues

As I hear
the slushy sound of wheels
through pools of water,
the morning is awash.

Not with sunlight,
but with heaven's bounty
that settles the dust
in our lives.

Everything is still,
having enjoyed the downpour;
like a newborn
fast asleep, freshly bathed.

This constant renewal
of nature is the oxygen
of our lives;
we need these changes,
to sustain ourselves.

Responding
to nature's moods,
we change ours.
At present, I want to hug you.

Partner Me

☙

You, the comfort of my life,
the one that will sustain;
friend, lover, philosopher,
you helped me live again.

Creasing doubts lurked within,
my thoughts in quarantine,
you never let me feel alone,
cleared cobwebs from my being.

You were the Jhansi of my life,
battling courageously;
conflicts devoured me within,
fought all my mutinies.

The present pounds within my heart,
the past, within my mind,
helped savour many memories,
my equilibrium find.

Greener Pastures

May solitude be
a distant
dream,
the fragrance
of petals
celebrating life,
embracing
its munificence.

No more those
grassless patches
in wilderness,
leading to
nowhere.

Time to hold
your hand
and walk
silently
in peace.

What's in a Name

My name is like
my number plate,
attached to me,
just like my fate.

Think of one
Hazara Singh
Lakha Singh
one Piara Singh.

Or think perhaps
of Kirori Mal
Mehnga Ram
Tijori Mal.

Names have stories
not often told;
the following one
let me unfold:

Jolly and Puppy,
a happy pair,
going through life
without a care.

Their first born
the Lucky one,

both Happy
with another son.

Sweety then came,
a joyous gift
gave their spirits
a sudden lift.

Living life
with no regret
then came Tommy,
their precious pet.

Sweety, Happy
and Lucky grew,
a Jolly delicious
family brew.

Lucky made
a Cheeky choice,
a new addition,
another voice.

Puppy felt
Cheeky was brash,
drain on surplus
family cash.

Kitty parties
every week,
expensive habits,
pleasures seek.

Persuaded Happy
to choose Goldy,
family business
in diamond jewelry.

The Goldy-Cheeky
axis soured
family peace,
jilted and scarred.

Sweety now
had come of age,
the Lovely boy,
a local rage.

Gave in dowry
guinea pounds,
in-laws owners
of godowns.

Happy, Lucky
in deep sorrow,

tell sister Sweety
manage somehow.

Tell your husband
to find a house,
you want to live
alone with spouse.

Well recognised
by all today,
must adopt, embrace
new modern ways.

The yuppies of
our nouveau class
face conflicts of
the bahu-saas.

The changing ways
of modern life,
caught between
mother and wife.

Our middle class,
amidst success,
full of turmoil,
tension and stress.

In this crass
commercial world,
traditional values
hard to hold.